Poppies In The Sand

By
Ramona Swift-Thiessen

www.xulonpress.com

Appreciations

"*R*amona has written a book full of God's love and faithfulness. This book will inspire, encourage, and lead you deep into His love and His words of promise for you."

Cathy Ferrell
Internationally acclaimed,
award winning Sculptor
Florida, USA

"Those on a spiritual path will recognize all the ups and downs, twists and turns wc all experience on this marvellous journey called life. This book will surely find its way to those who will benefit by its reading. *Poppies in the Sand* will make a thoughtful gift book from one friend to another!"

Pam Dean Cable
Executive Director of the
Susan Kathleen Black Foundation
Colorado, USA

"I have known Ramona for several years now, meeting her first at an artist workshop in Montana. She struck me as a woman of many talents – painting, singing and song writing being just a few. Like most people, Ramona's life has had some wrinkles. *Poppies In the Sand* reflects on some of those wrinkles and outlines her journey of finding peace, spirituality and most importantly, a feeling of hope.

Sit back and enjoy the prose, whether you believe in yourself or something bigger, there is always room for hope."

Terry Isaac
Internationally acclaimed Wildlife artist
British Columbia, Canada

Contents

Dedication

*T*hank you to my son, Nathan, for hanging in there and keeping our home one of laughter and fun. You always have been such a joyful part of my days.

Thank you Mom and Dad for praying with me and just loving me. My brother Kevin and sister-in-law Shelley for including us in so many family gatherings and your lives, in general, for our first two years in Saskatchewan. Your home is a place of safety and love.

Thank you Carol my big sister (though you are actually small). You are the Bible scholar of the bunch and your words of life and encouragement gave me strength.

Denise, my email angel who wrote amazing letters to me. You are like Aaron, holding up Moses arms when he was too tired to hold them any longer on his own. When I was low, you always lifted me up.

Thank you Cary for the love I never knew possible. I feel so blessed to know you. You have my heart forever.

To everyone who may see their part in my story, thank you, too. My mind is scanning to recall all those who spoke wise counsel to me, or gave a helping hand: Al, Bonnie, Gary, Diane,

Ken, Linda, Daren and Kristen. I know there are so many more. Each of you are significant and mean the world to me! Thank you.

It's time to put together the vignettes and stories that have been snapshots of how adversity in life can grow depth, character, beauty and give many answers. Impurities, in precious metals, come through the refiner's firing process, and something good can transpire even when ugly things in life are confronting us.

This book is a compilation of thoughts pondered, insights gathered and hope restored due to the deepening faith that has developed through my own refiner's fire.

Life gives each of us defining moments. Taken wrongly, they can define you into a victim. They can define your spirit into a bitter, forever-wounded, always grieving person. Or taken rightly, in our broken state and given to our heavenly Father, they can define you into a victor; a joyful loving person with a winning spirit, filled with hope for the future. They can be what turn you from fickle to solid, shallow to deep, unstable to committed and dependable.

You can go from coasting along in your life, feeling ungrateful, to seeing things with new eyes. Eyes that appreciate those who love you. Those things in your care that you may have considered drudgeries can be seen as precious and lovely.

1

Beautiful Strength

O’ve always been attracted to things in nature that are beautiful in spite of adversity, or maybe because of adversity. It seems a reflection of what people are like. Those who live a life with no challenges become small-minded. They can be harsh in their judgments on others. Anyone who has been through a lot; some kind of crisis or suffered grief from loss, usually will have learned how to let the small petty stuff go. Things are put into perspective when a loved one dies or is sick, or you face foreclosure on your home, or your marriage is dissolving, or a child is heading the wrong direction in life.

We also have those life breathed scriptures that say the Lord draws near to the broken hearted, those crushed in spirit (Psalm 34:18). It becomes more than words on a page when it is your own heart that is broken; *your* spirit that feels crushed into shards.

It all began on a hot summer's day in the Okanagan Valley, British Columbia. I put on my ipod that I always had downloaded with books by inspirational speakers. I usually never got started on my hikes until it was close to 10:00am when the summer sun was already throwing some intense heat. As I passed by the local gravel pit one typical morning, my eyes locked on to what seemed an impossible thing. A small cluster of bright red, wild poppies on their fragile little stems were growing out of the side of the sandy gravel heap. It appeared as if nothing was holding them there. They were the only splash of color and it was desert dry. The title to this book was thought of that day, four years ago.

Poppies have been something that I am constantly amazed at, drawn to, passionate about painting and give me such joy. Just gazing at them on a sunny day, when their petals let the light shine through, changing the colors from red to gold and brilliant orange, sends my senses into orbit!

When I saw those poppies in the gravel pit, another phrase came to mind and it was "shine where you are". They were doing that in a living illustration. Like a person who has come from humble beginnings, who realizes their purpose and shines with excellence.

It is my purpose in this book to encourage the readers to believe that no matter what is thrown your way, whether self-inflicted or by others; you are able to rise above. You can be all that God your maker intended you to be, and do all He intended for you to do. Only you can get in the way of those plans, not anyone else or anything. Times along the way may seem impossible and dry, but they are the middle of the journey, not the end. Keep reading. Let me share some of my story and thoughts with you.

2

You are Here to be Light

"You are here to be light, bringing out the God colors in the world. God is not a secret to be kept. We are going public with this! As public as a city on a hill! As light bearers you don't think I'm going to hide you under a bucket do you? I'm putting you on a light stand. Now that I've put you there on a hill top on a light stand, Shine!" Matthew 5:14-16 (Message Translation)

I love these verses! They are my statement as an artist! There is more to what I do than painting something to match the curtains nicely! There is punch, power and God's got a purpose! It's bigger than me! That's why when the poppies have barren sand all around them, when the rain hasn't come for awhile, and the scorching sun is beating down, they are not destroyed! Only God can say when their time is up.

Meanwhile, they do what they were put on earth to do...grow and shine!

When I am wanting to paint a scene that is

incredibly detailed it can appear to be an over-
whelming project. In order to manage it, and
focus on a piece at a time, I literally block off all
but the area I'm working on at the time. I cover
up the part I'm not wanting to think about at that
moment with paper. It's like baby steps really. You
can't do everything at once. Can't do everything
you want to accomplish in a day. If we get frus-
trated because we want to do something spectac-
ular and of eternal significance it's a way to think
about things too. The 'to do' list can be paralyzing
and shift your focus off of what God wants you to
focus on. That is, "Seek first His kingdom (His will
"what do you have for me today?) and all these
things will be added to you. (insert mine).

Get moving
Just get started
Baby steps if you need to
Put on your sneakers
Comb your hair
Wash your face and get moving
If it's a task, just start
The taste of accomplishment
Has a wonderful flavour.
If it is writing someone you are
Thinking of
Get out the paper.
Seeing it complete in the sealed stamped
envelope
Will be fulfilling!
If it's a million things you have to do
Well make a list and then start doing.
One by one
Step by step

The list will get shorter
And make sure to have a great cup of
Coffee (or tea)
For the prize at the end
Because
You did good
You got moving!

I have had a few blindsides and disappointments in life. They seem to strategically follow something wonderful. One time in particular I was about to begin the biggest project of my artist career at the time. It was a commission to do an 11foot high 9ft wide triptych painting of a waterfall. It would be a benchmark for me. I knew it came from the hand of God as a gift. The huge canvases arrived and were hauled downstairs to my studio. It is difficult to describe how exciting that was! Each one alone was larger than any single painting I'd ever tackled, let alone three to create one image! I had barely begun, and one morning was skipping down the stairs to work on them. I know it sounds like a Susie Sunshine thing, but I truly had a song in my heart because I felt so blessed. Only days into it, my husband of 25 plus years told me he no longer knew if he wanted to be married to me. We had experienced many things over the years, but he had never said such a thing as this to me before. I thought that after all we'd been through, we would always be together. I remembered that day as 'black Sunday'. Things ceased to move. People who have these kinds of things come at them, can relate to the sense that the earth and everything in it has stopped cold. Suddenly nothing matters that seemed to be important even moments before. Appetite - gone. Sleep? - non-existent. Motivation? Out the window!

Many Bible passages over the years have really been there to penetrate my heart when its feeling wounded. Here is one that just pulled me. It is in Psalms. A book full of prayers and proclamations from a poet/king in the Bible. "The Lord draws near to the broken hearted and saves those who are crushed in spirit." Psalms 34:18

As I began what I could to get through those days and work on the painting instead of withdrawing from life, I had to change some things. I could no longer listen to anything I wanted to. I didn't want to take the chance to happen upon a love song, or worse yet, a break up song. That would have left me in a puddle on the floor. It had to be inspirational, worship music. That is all I listened to for the entire duration of the waterfall painting. It helped me immensely. God's presence was there abundantly. He could see around the corners I could not. All I could see was the picture I had of our life disappearing, and there being nothing I could do to save it. God saw further. He still had plans for me. Good plans too, but life happens to people.

So He loved me. He put my name in people's minds and they would be there for me without my asking. He drew near. It was still painful. I cried. I battled through the night without sleep and I lost weight because I could not eat.

Today looking back, I am amazed at the strength only God could have given me to paint such a project, and to be a mom to my son during that time. He even gave me wonderful snapshot moments of peace and laughter. I have journaled those special times.

One friend asked me what she could do for me. I was trying to paint and still live in the same house as my husband who no longer wanted to be married. It was hard to focus in the tension. I asked her if I could use her workshop. She was out of the country for the winter, but said "yes" in a heartbeat. She said she'd have her landscaper bring me the keys to the gate and her house would be mine for as long or whenever I needed it. If I wanted to sleep there, I could. I love her. It was an impossible thing to dare to feel like I was in any way suffering when I sat down on the private dock overlooking the magnificent lake with the view of mountains in the distance.

Such peace inhabited that property. God was there. He helped me paint something more than a blackened canvas, which was all I felt I would be able to do.

The painting latcr was named "Ilealing Waters." It seemed appropriate.

Me feet are in sand and its keeping me bogged.
I cannot move forward
I cannot sleep, eat,
Or rest.
Oh God...You hear me when I pray.
You promise to be close to the broken hearted and save those who are crushed in spirit.
That is me right now.
This is so hurtful, so lonely.
Answer me and lift me up as you promised. Out of the slippery clay.
Put my feet on a rock. Give me footing. Give me rest.
Fill my spirit with hope; with peace.
I know you can bring about good changes
Out of bad circumstances.
My confidence is in You.
Blanket me in your peace.
Amen

3

Provision

*G*od has been my great provider. All that I have ever enjoyed came from His hand. But, you know how we think. We bemoan that we have to get up out of bed in the morning, forgetting that the bed itself is a provision! We get to have a bed with blankets, under a roof. We get to go to sleep safely behind a closed door. We work hard and get tired. We get paid, and we forget that even the job we have is a gift from Him. We forget to be grateful.

When you have two incomes, it is even easier to forget that you need God because you have a pretty consistent source of income. You have credit cards. You have a line of credit. It's much like a fog that lets you imagine everything is fine. You will have what you need and eventually, someday, will magically be out of debt!

When I found myself on my own, the fog quickly cleared! With clarity, I saw what the reality was. I had no line of credit or overdraft protection to get me through a month of sparse income. I had credit card debt far beyond what was smart. No credit card debt is smart, but I am embarrassed at the amount I had on the two cards in my possession.

I also had a bought a new house one month

before becoming the sole wage earner to pay it each month. Bam! My knees hit the floor and the prayers started with much less eloquence than when things are going easy. It was more like, "God, help me! I need you!"

Since that very heartfelt, humble prayer and honest assessment of how things were, God has provided financial miracles every month. I have always had enough. It has been amazing, and all I have to do to remember He is alive and real is to tell someone what I do for an occupation! I am currently making minimum wage as a part time waitress. As an artist, I have no idea what I'll make month to month.

It's a good and a bad thing to have these types of jobs. Good because you pray a lot! Good because there is no cap on the salary as far as what I might make in tips or in art sales. Bad because I could make no sales and very low tips. On my income as a waitress, I could not make the mortgage payment. Let alone pay the power bill, phone bill, other utilities, buy groceries for a teenager and myself and fuel for my truck. However, not once has that been the case. Requests for commissioned art work have come in, prints and paintings have sold without having booked a show, traveled or advertised. Amazing!

Here is what I think is the key. It's my secret!

Actually, it's not a secret at all and many people I respect and admire do this and believe in it. It's tithing, or setting apart 10% of my income from each check I get and giving it back to God to show my thanks.

I think God wants to see if we are faithful in the little things. If we are stingy with 10% of our small income, He will keep that income small. We cannot be trusted with His generosity. Wealth could ruin us if we are greedy with the little. Know this though; God does not need our money! His is the wealth of the world. He is God. He doesn't go to stores or pay a mortgage. He does control the universe. He does see a generous heart and a faithful heart and He rewards that.

A pastor once said to think of the tithe as the root of your money. If you give God's work the 10 percent, it is protection for that root. If the root is protected, the rest will flourish.

If I never experienced any results or saw unexpected income show up, I may be able to be convinced it isn't true. But I have seen way too much to ever change my mind about it now.

This subject is dear to my heart because when I lay in my comfy bed at night, when I hear the buzz of the refrigerator and the furnace kick in on a cold winter's night, I know that these comforts are mine because God provides. I am His daughter and He is pleased that I have read His words and believed them. The law of provision and blessing is in His word many times. I believe them and if you want to see some miraculous things, I highly recommend tithing. You will see!

4

Thought Life

❦

Napoleon Hill says adamantly in his book, "Think and Grow Rich" that the good Lord gave us control over one thing and one thing only. That one thing is our thoughts. He was drilling in the fact that you are also the only person who can change your thoughts. I am least productive if I let my mind dwell on things that make me angry or spend time remembering hurts. Even current things that are irritating me can absolutely put me at a standstill creatively. Simple day to day tasks can take longer than they should when negative thoughts are allowed to take up residence in my mind.

2 Corinthians 10:5 was a scripture I learned to repeat and pray. It was necessary several times a day when my mind became a battlefield of negative thoughts. "We demolish arguments and every pretension that sets itself up against the knowledge of God and we take captive every thought to make it obedient to Christ."

My Dad was an interesting example of how to handle negative thoughts and conflict as I was growing up. I never remember he and my Mom having any big verbal fights. I would know that

25

there was a disagreement from time to time, but Dad would go out to the shop and build something when he was stewing about an issue. I laugh now to remember how many little horseshoe carrying cases he had built and stacked up in the workshop! He would always be whistling a song. These were songs I recognized as hymns. It is a hard thing for a mind to hold opposite moods at the same time. It seems incapable of nursing a dark and brooding thought, and singing or whistling an uplifting song at the same time. Good strategy Dad! To this day, I try to sing songs or recite verses I've memorized to keep my mind in the right place and be positive.

5

Worst Year Ever/maybe not

I had started a journal in 2010. I picked it up and was thumbing through it the other day. It seemed to be the worst year of my life. As I read through it, I found out it was also the best year of my life.

It was a year unlike any other; a turning point to everything I'd come to know as normal. I learned, in 2010, to pray on a whole new level. I was also given gift after gift from people! These were not jewels and money that I'm talking about. Getting to go to a Joyce Meyers conference in Spokane with a girlfriend on my birthday and being treated to supper at the Olive Garden is a sample of the sweetness I experienced.

It wasn't unusual to wander over to the computer in the morning, with my cup of coffee, and still wearing my pajamas, to find an email saying someone wanted to buy a painting. So, before even getting dressed that day, I could say I made $1500.00. That's an awesome beginning to anyone's day. I also want to add that these sales were not from people who knew of what was going on in my life. They were not sympathy sales, which made them so exciting to me. In 2010, I won a scholarship to an artist workshop in Dubois, Wyoming, sold 19 original paintings, 2 of which were of the massive size, and got a beautiful truck, fully funded by sales in artwork.

God provided me with what I called my 'midnight angels' with my sister and another friend who he'd wake up in the night to write me emails that breathed hope and encouragement back into me. My sleep patterns were disrupted for about a year. I'd battle with bouts of fear and pain and would have to just get up out of bed before it consumed me. That's when I'd start the computer up, and there would be letters from those two angels! They were always filled with encouragement, promises of good things from the word of God...lots of hope.

Neither of them remembers exactly what they wrote, and sadly, I did not keep the letters, but they were breath from God to my lungs.

My brother and his wife whisked my son and I off to come see them over the school's Spring Break that year and we experienced a little oasis from all the chaos for two weeks. There are so many things to remember of people being the hands, feet and voices of my heavenly Father to me. Friends saying, "Let's pray", as we sat in the pickup truck together in a driveway, sending me off with hope in my heart, and a feeling of being covered.

Then there are the little treasures. These are things I wrote down to remember. One day, feeling very dejected and alone, I decided to sit in the hot tub we had on our deck. Our house was for sale because of our marriage dissolving and I just felt so sad. I went to my room to change clothes, and when I came out, my son, who was fourteen at the time, stood with two cans of frosty cold cokes in his hands. I remember he was wearing swimming shorts and mismatched socks and had this quirky grin on his face, asking if I wanted company. I'd planned to go out there alone and just be sad. Instead, it was a nice time with company. Sweet little treasures to not be overlooked. The list goes on and on. It was a very good year all in all. You don't get to see the good in people sometimes in its fullest capacity until there is a need for it to be exposed.

6

Strive for Excellence

This is another godly principle. It is not the same as perfectionism. Perfectionism keeps things from getting done. I've seen it way too often. You want to do everything. You want perfect conditions, perfect results. If it can't be perfect, you don't even start. As a result, you have this big pride thing about how you are a perfectionist, and...that's all you have. You have nothing but a title of pride and it's not *anything* to be proud of! The Bible tells us to work as unto the Lord. If you were doing a painting for God, or making a meal for Him, or washing a car for Him, you'd do it really well. You'd do it with all your might...every detail would be carefully noticed. Excellence starts in the heart. You think of others and want to do an excellent job for the pleasure of someone else.

That's very different than the other standard "What's in it for me?"

I want God to be pleased with the work of my hands. I want Him to say, "Well Done." In the same way He views our lives, He doesn't expect perfection. He does tell us to work on our skills. "See a man who is skilled in his work? He will serve before Kings. He will not be obscure..." Proverbs

22:29. I'd be okay with hearing what a king would have me paint for his castle! Therefore, I will work on my skills. I will strive for excellence, but I will work regardless of whether the circumstances are perfect. Remember the poppies in the gravel pit? They would never have grown if conditions needed to be perfect to get started.

7

Laziness/Poverty

I gravitate towards the sections in the library where books on business, motivation, selling strategies, marketing plans are. I like books that amp a person up and get them excited about possibilities if they apply themselves. I found one book that broke down and dissected the book of Proverbs. It is one of the best I've ever read to help me see answers to every business question I've faced thus far. It changed my life and I'd recommend it to everyone. It is Stephen K. Scott's book, "The Richest Man who ever Lived."

I never have been one to just wait for things to come to me. If anything, I err on the side of trying to push things to happen maybe before the timing is just right, and need to learn to be more patient. But I have been around way too many talented people who think that great things should just come to them. One day, they'll get their lucky break and they just...wait. There is a certain arrogance to that attitude. Maybe be willing to fly economy class before you get that first class ticket. Get up, show some initiative and work diligently.

8

Forgiveness

*T*oday, my mind did battle over things I could not control. Ever have a day like that? I have them often. Circumstances had arisen, which caused ripple effects to those around the decision maker. I grappled with praying things like the Psalmist did on some of his bad days. "God, smite the offender with boils. May everything he touches fail, burn up or die!" Lovely thoughts like that! It doesn't sound too lovely or Christian of me, but it's real. I am real.

Then my wonderfully patient dad told me that I needed to focus instead on the things in my life that are good. Things God has given me. He is right, of course.

Feelings are not to be denied necessarily, but they can be channeled and directed. It is easy to find a friend that will chime right in with you in all your negative talk and thoughts. Sometimes, that just feels too good to let pass by. But, if you want to grow, if you want to prosper in spirit, it isn't the long term answer. Truthfully, it isn't even the short term answer! The right thing and the best 'revenge' is to carry on and live the life God intended for you; discover your gifts, love and serve people. Get way past all those negative things that weigh you down. Think of them as cement shoes that keep you from running the race, that keep you from winning. Imagine how great it will feel to take those shoes off, and be able to run feeling as light as air!

Happiness is an elusive word, and I think in our quest, it should be replaced with the word "joy". Joy is different than happiness because happy is quick, and most often dictated by circumstances, to exist. Joy can sit there in your heart no matter what the debris around you may look like. No matter what people are saying. In spite of what the balance in your bank account is; joy is deeper and will keep you stable on the rockiest of ground. I'll take joy.

Let the bad stuff go and be thankful for the life God has given you. Put good things in your mind. Choose carefully what you let yourself read or watch on the screen.

I am preaching to myself as I write! Can you tell? To be told to 'just forgive' seemed to me to mean, 'sweep under the carpet, paint over, or hide the book under your bed.' It doesn't though. I have felt the difference in my stomach! I think because unforgiveness is bitter, it literally can cause a bitter acid in your stomach. I don't have medical proof, only the feeling of being sick inside, and losing my appetite. My life experience is my only proof. Brilliant people have explained things much better than I can, but I do know that bitterness causes illness. It takes sleep away. It steals joy! How, I wondered, can you forgive when it might mean, to the other person who hurt you, they are off the hook?

Well, *why* is the more important question. Why? Because you want a good part two to your life. I'm not sure why we want to just wallow in the pain long after the fact. I know there is this strange part in us that says such things as "I deserve to feel this way!" There is some stupid kind of comfort in replaying everything that was ever done wrong to you and eating a gallon of ice-cream while you do it. Which, by the way, will only depress you more when you come down from the sugar rush and realize you also just gained ten pounds. Now you are fat on top of being depressed, angry and bitter! It's just not a good way to go!

Again, my help came from the Lord and verses that I've read. The one that I printed out and came to me often is Jeremiah 29:11. *"For I know the plans I have for you. Plans to prosper and not to harm you. Plans for hope and a future."* When I thought about that and allowed those words to come to life for me, I decided I did want a good life. Even if it was different than the one I'd believed I'd have. Even if I were alone. I wanted the full deal. If God had something in mind for me that was good, abundant, and full, I wanted it. I had to drop the bag at the gate though. The bag of unforgiveness cannot pass through the gate where hope and a new future await.

9

Encourage and Refresh Others

He who refreshes others will be him-self refreshed. Proverbs 11:25

I have a whole mental Rolodex of cool stories on the fun of giving when prompted by God. They are not stories of being able to give a room full of people new cars. But in scale to who I am and what I have, they are my experiences with that same kind of wonderful.

One day, I was sitting on a bench, out in my garden, having some time with God. It was a place I loved to go in the summer mornings to pray. This particular morning, nothing lovely was making its way into my heart. I could see the but-terflies flitting from flower to flower, the petals in brilliant colors. It didn't lift me as it usually did. So, I prayed a prayer like this: "God, I do not want to be so inward. All my thoughts are going to the same dark place. I want to be outward and think of others. I want to be an encouragement to someone, but don't feel like I can be in this state of mind. Today, can you help me find someone who needs encouragement? Tell me how to give them something or say the right thing that You want me to. P.S. say it loud because I might not hear You if You whisper."

That day, I went into town to pick up some canvases and frames I'd had made at the framing shop. There was a girl there named T.J. She was always one I knew if you gave a job to, she'd do it well. She took pride in her work and was thorough. I didn't know a lot about her other than I could always count on her to do a job well, and have the answers for me when I asked.

With zero intention to do anything but pick up my order, I walked into the building that morning. Funny how God does not forget such a prayer as I'd prayed that morning. He loves those kinds of prayers because He is always working and He sees many people besides yourself; people who might be praying something like "God, if You are real, I need You to show me today that You even know and care that I am down here."

I was standing at the counter and TJ was writing up my invoice. A voice...not audible, more like a thought in bold font, came into my head. It was not of my own.

God: Ramona, I want you to give TJ your ring.

Me: What?!

God: I choose TJ. You asked me this morning who needed encouragement.

Me: My ring God? I love this ring! (It was a wide band of cool hammered silver. It had the words, *be true to your dreams*, on it.)

God: Give TJ your ring. Tell her I told you to.

Me: I barely know her. She will think I'm crazy!

God: *So?*

The feeling was so strong; I could not hear anything else. It was almost as though I had a headset on, drowning out all other noises and voices. I knew I was hooped until I followed through.

I said, (gulp) "TJ?"

TJ was a busy girl and was working away. She said, "Yep" and never looked up.

I said, "I'd like to give you something. (pause) I have never done anything like this, but I feel really strongly like I should."

She said, "(still crunching numbers and typing. She was listening but her focus was on the paperwork) Uh huh."

I went on, "So, I'm going to take it off now..."

TJ stopped typing and looked up with a "what are you doing" look on her face.

I said, "I want to give you my ring", and I passed it to her. She instantly put it on her finger and, of course, it fit her perfectly.

She said, "Are you serious?! Why would you do this? I love it!" (it was a *really* cool ring I must emphasize!)

I said, "Well, with some things I am going through right now, separating from my husband, having to move, sell things that are important to me, it's easy to get very inwardly focused. I don't want to become a bitter angry woman. This morning I asked God to show me someone He wanted to encourage. I told Him He needed to say it loud because I might not hear it otherwise. Honestly, I haven't been able to hear anything else since I came in here! He said He chooses you and that He wants you to have this ring because... (swallow) because He loves you." (Now I want to run because I am sure she is going to look at me like I have ten heads and think I'm insane for admitting I heard a voice while I was standing there in front of her).

It went quite differently. She came around the counter and gave me a big hug. She had tears in her eyes and said, "I have been wondering about that actually." She told me she loved it and would always wear it. Later, she told me again that it gave her a reason to smile many mornings as she thought about God picking her out of the people I knew or would see that day to give a present to. It was not me just randomly giving to the first person I saw. It was asking God to direct me to a person who needed to know He loved them; He saw them.

T.J. was a single mom of 3 children. Her life had been hard, and she had experienced losing her house and the load of responsibility to keep her young family together, clothed and fed. She had to struggle and work tirelessly to support them. She was a fighter and a survivor. But fighters and survivors still get weary and need encouragement.

Those are cool things when you cross over the line from hesitation to obedience. They are wow moments you don't forget.

There are many and each equally important and special in my heart. Some, I learned a lesson right away or saw the reason. Some, I never have gotten to see the reaction or impact as I was impressed to do something anonymously. I do know that this day, in particular, I felt I came away with much more than I had given.

Silver Boxes
Given freely
But of such value
Words of kindness
Of edifying
Praise, encouragement
Given with tenderness
Resulting in power
To the receiver
Life giving
Lung-filling
Heart swelling words
Amazing
Silver boxes
Handed gently
Sincerely over
To someone we care about
And there is no expiry date
On the effective
Positive results
Costing us nothing
Except some thought
Some compassion
Maybe some time to do it
But so worth the effort

10

Keep Your Word

$\mathcal{B}$eing a person of your word is so important. Don't allow little things you promised to go undone, even if no one mentions them to you. Chances are they are not forgotten and your reputation can go south, even just a little. It's not a good thing to get in the habit of not doing.

One example in my life was one night when I wasn't sleeping. I wandered out to check my emails and somehow stumbled upon an old one between myself and a client. This was the lady who had commissioned me to paint the waterfall painting I spoke of earlier. This letter was written before we had it fully figured out if I'd take the job, price and other details. I'd written, "If I do this painting, when it is finished, we should have a big unveiling party/show at your place. It would be a great opportunity for people to see your B&B, as well as for me to show/sell some other work," and I added, "I would give you 15% of all the sales I made that day for having it at your place."

When I read that, I gasped. I had not remembered saying that. But there it was and by now, I'd done the painting and had the show! The 15% commission hadn't been mentioned by either of us.

I wondered why I had said 15% of all sales when usually I paid that for sales of originals, and I badly needed the money. I was getting packed and ready to move. My future was uncertain. I decided that I needed to keep my word no matter what. Even if the clients were not mentioning it to me, I figured it was because of my personal situation they'd decided not to bother reminding me. I thought, "I guess I will just have to trust God to somehow, through some other means, make up for what I'm writing this check out for." I added up all the sales and wrote the check. It'd been a good show and so the amount was big for me to give up. I really sensed that one day that amount would not seem as big to me, as it did that day.

I went up to their place to see them and gave the itemized list of things sold, down to the last note card and included the check totaling 15% of the amount on the list.

Robby had been a vice-principal of a high school for years. She perused my note with sharp piercing eyes, and then the check as only someone in that position could, and I was nervous. I felt like she was checking it for math errors!

Suddenly, she ripped the check to shreds and said very firmly, "That show was our gift to you! There is no way we will accept payment for it!"

I just burst into tears. The outcome was not at all expected. I'd been given the entire amount back and still had been able to be a woman of my word. Times like that were a lesson to me. In business and in your personal life, don't make promises you do not make every effort to keep. If you cannot keep them, don't avoid the topic. Bring it out in the open and talk about alternative options. Be upfront and trustworthy.

11

Faith and Fear

*S*ometimes faith comes easy. Sometimes it is much more of a struggle, depending on how much pressure is on me.

Recently, I felt a lot of pressure financially. I had a couple of days before my first art show of the year. I felt pressure to have it do well, to sell paintings, prints and build up my account again. It had reached its lowest balance since I'd been on my own.

Fear wanted to enter my mind and heart. I kept working at pushing 'him' out the door, reminding myself of how I've always had all of my needs met. There has always been enough and when I've prayed and followed the principles of God, I have seen the promises unfold for me and my son.

One day, I prayed something like this, "God, I've done all I know to do. I've given you 10% of my income from every source it's come in. I've worked with a heart striving for excellence. I've given extra or been obedient to do what You asked if I felt You prompting me. Now, I need You to move in again and do something supernatural. George Mueller never asked anyone for money. He just asked You and You provided year after year for him and all the orphanages he ran. It is the way I want it to be here. So there is no way I can take the credit for making something happen. I would love for You to put me on someone's heart. We need some money soon. So, I'm asking. Simple as that."

I did my best to just walk away then and trust that it was taken care of. There was a pesky little fly of doubt buzzing around my head though. I confess I am not a pillar of faith. I have what I have, and offer that.

The very next day I got an email from someone I have not been in contact with since I moved away. We had limited contact when I lived there too, to be honest. She wrote me a very short email. It went like this:

"Ramona, I would like to have your address as there is a gift I would like to send you. Better yet, could you give me your account number and information? You have been strongly on my mind since yesterday and I feel like I am supposed to give you some money. I want to follow this prompting because I feel it is from God."

Are you saying, "No way!" with me? That is specific isn't it? That's an answer that shows that God hears us when we pray and we can go to Him with our cares. It isn't coincidental. It isn't positive thinking. It was too timely, too specific to be. She had no idea what I'd prayed. No one but God did.

Freedom lives on the other side of fear
But Fear will do its best
To block your path
At your every attempt
To advance.
Freedom has no walls
Or fences,
Only rolling hills of
Green;
Possibilities , peaceful sleeps,
Positive and happy thoughts,
Boundless energy, the purest love.
Fear is the border crossing.
It patrols the crossing
With diligence, fierceness and angst
There is no letting up.
The reason why is simple.
It knows no one
Ever returns to cross back
Once they taste the freedom side of the road.

12

Planning for the Future

*P*lan for the future, but live like today is the destiny you were put here for. Just in case it is going to be awhile before you get to where you really want to be, don't waste all your time pining away for something better.

I will always be a dreamer. It is my nature to be a dreamer and I like that part of me. My imagination comes up with original things when I am painting or writing songs or poetry.

The reality is that you will see promotion and be recognized for great things sooner if you are your best self right where you are today. Today is important. How you treat people *today* matters.

Today, if you are prompted to give someone something, do it. It may be a note of encouragement. It may be paying for someone's coffee or breakfast. If you are better set financially, it may be something bigger like paying for someone less privileged to go to college!

It is for a reason though. It will continually make you more and more sensitive to the needs of others and to the voice of God. Don't let your heart harden. You cannot excel, cannot fulfill your destiny, or live your dreams if you deviate

from making the day you are living and breathing
a day of its greatest value.

Cherish
The days you have
The ones you love
The life you live

Relish
In the warmth of the sun
The refreshing of the rain
The love of a friend

Delight
In small pleasures
In lovely blessings
In solid relationships

Extend
Encouragement to another
Show them they matter
Bless them in some way

13

Wilderness Times

*H*ave you even known, or sensed, there was something amazing coming for you? Do you love success stories about actors or singers who tell of having to sleep in their cars or eat left-overs from room service in hotels to survive before they got their big break?

I love the ones who just kept going, kept believing that even though times were tough and presently didn't look like any kind of success story; they could not let go of the dream. I recall reading that one very well known actor wrote a check out for a million dollars and said that one day he'd be able to do that and the check would be good! That did come true many times over for him! (Guaranteed he did not just wait and have it happen without any effort!)

Dolly Parton wrote, in her autobiography, that she used to eat the food people left outside of their hotel room doors when she was a struggling singer/songwriter. Many of them were waiters, waitresses, played in dives, but always planning to one day do more. Always believing if they were diligent, things would improve.

This does tie into the last entry. I love how the

Bible describes times like these as wilderness times. Times like when the children of Israel had wandered in the desert eating the same thing, morning noon and night, for what seemed forever! All before they reached the Promised Land. David was anointed to be the future king by the prophet Samuel, but it took years before it transpired. Meanwhile, there were times he was running for his life by the reigning and jealous king at the time. David had to live in caves when he'd been promised a castle!

Those were wilderness times. Perhaps when Joseph was in the pit, or later in jail, he felt the longing for his previous dreams to come true. There is a preparation taking place in wilderness times though. Character is being shaped, faith is being developed. Learning to seek God, hear God, depend on God is being developed.

At one point in the Exodus story, the children of Israel were wailing and complaining about how much they hated the manna that was being provided for them every day. They wanted MEAT! God heard (He wasn't happy that they were saying it the way they were; wailing that they would rather be back in Egypt and they loathed that useless manna!), but He said He would give them meat. Moses cried out, "Where am I supposed to find meat for all these people?" Note the mistake in that? God was the supplier, not Moses. God is the one who made the promise and would be the one to bring it to pass.

I go to these stories to strengthen my resolve. I like to remember that it is not just me and my dreamer self wanting to go to another level with my art, and with whatever other gifts I'd like to see developed further and utilized. These were planted in me at birth by my maker! He is the one who can bring them to pass (do I hear an amen?)

So, when you find yourself in the wilderness, remember these stories. He does not see hills of sand and gravel. He sees the glorious glowing poppies! He sees you as you WILL be and if you are willing, and if you ask Him, there is nothing He wants more than to help you see it come to be.

Do not lose hope. Do not give up. Hang on and believe that God has good plans for you. He made you with a selection and special combination of gifts that no one else has. They are like your own fingerprint. He sees you. He knows you by name. Choose to believe that and stop struggling. Just ask Him and listen for the answers. Take quiet time and learn to be still sometimes. You hear best when the clutter and noise is held back even if just for small segments of time. It is as worth it as stopping to sharpen your saw when cutting wood. If you arc too busy to sharpen the saw, the task will take much longer than it should.

I press on
Even when it's boring
I press on
I dig in
And push myself
Because that is what
Will make the difference
That is what will
Separate me from the rest
If I press on
When I don't want to.
When I want a day off
Because what I want more
Than a day off,
Is to be great at this
Passion of mine;
To soar to places
I dream about.
To know that I did
What I could to squeeze
Out every ounce of my
God-given potential and hopefully
Get a little more
Along the way.
SO I PRESS ON.

14

Refiner's Fire

*W*e can be defined by the sad things, or tragedies, in our lives. One of the very prominent gravel pits of my life was the wish to have children. After being married two years, I just assumed we would be able to make the decision that 'now' was the time and begin our family. Like a lot of girls, I started imagining what the children might look like and what names I'd give them, I dreamed about their looks, personalities, talents etc. Year after year passed. More of my friends and cousins got married and had one, two and three children. Still, we had none. Finally, the fertility tests were checked into. Then I went through a second round of them. Finally, we began to consider the more expensive and extensive approaches. All to no avail.

One day, I got a call that changed my life. We had not ever applied to adopt a child and suddenly were being asked if we would adopt a three month old baby boy. We had this wonderful child in our home with us within three days of that phone call and life has never been the same! As I write this, my sixteen year old son's 6' tall frame is stretched out in a leather chair in the living room. He is drinking a liter sized glass of milk! Hmmm, my grocery bill has never been the same either!

After his arrival, many attempts were made to have a sibling for Nathan. More fertility treatments, applications to adopt and even foster. Nothing seemed to work out. We thought we were on a hot streak when we were told about a fifteen year old girl who was looking for the right family to give her baby to when it was born.

We went through all the case study meetings, interviews, paid money to a lawyer for the legal fees. When the baby was born, we were called to name him. Such an exciting time! We named him Matthew. In a couple of days, we were packed and heading to The Pas, MB to pick up our second baby boy! Nathan was three years old at this time. There was a ten day waiting period once we had the baby. This is when the mother can change her mind so we holed up in a little motel. The Pas was still having a brutal winter and the motel was chilly and dreary. But we were excited to get to day ten and head home. Day nine came, and we got a very upsetting phone call. The mother had changed her mind and decided to keep the baby in the family. At that time, it seemed like the ground came out from under my feet. We came home in a twenty hour car ride, with an empty car seat. We came home to a crib and a nursery filled with gifts from people who had been waiting to celebrate with us. There were also sympathy cards from those who'd been told by phone what had happened. It was such a dark time.

The pursuit carried on for a long time, to the point where I gave up long before my husband did. I wanted to stop striving and just enjoy having the one wonderful little boy we had. Eventually, he too decided this was the way it was going to be, so it was best to accept it. The alternative was just far too exhausting.

When Nathan was six years old, we got another out of the blue phone call. It was a request to take guardianship of my cousin's two children. The children were one and four years old. Things were on very shaky ground in their home and the parents said they were afraid they'd lose the children to social services. We understood that they were making a tough decision to have us adopt.

Taking them in meant completely flipping the life I had upside down and changing everything. I was a certified dog groomer and had a dog grooming business set up in my home. Nathan was in school full time, so I could work full days and contribute to our income. I quit the business the day before the children showed up.

It was a scary time for me. I'd never been a person who babysat other people's children. I wanted my own family and so, even after the children arrived, I struggled to have maternal feelings towards them, and also intense grief for not being more naturally wired that way. People continually were saying to us that we were so wonderful to be doing this for the kids and I felt like a huge hypocrite because I was feeling smothered and finding it so difficult. An artist needs/desires time alone and suddenly, I had none. Zero. Even the night times, the little one had to be in our room because he had nightmares. It was a difficult time on so many levels.

Eventually, after a few years, things seemed to be finding a stride. School helped as it freed up some time to allow me to breathe, to write, to paint. I did become a mother to them and loved them. I had become comfortable and felt they were indeed mine, in my heart. Then, they were taken away to return to their birth parents who had been working hard to reinvent their lives and make a more suitable environment for their children. They'd moved from their previous home and lived near us. It was difficult to let the kids go, but I knew that their mother's heart had been aching for their return. God made this plain to me in a dream that had a significant impact on how I could release them without having bitterness take root in my heart.

With all that had happened, it was a lovely gift from God that afterwards in the throes of sadness; He seemed to release a floodgate of paintings for me. They came to my mind, to my hand, to the canvas. He helped me grow at a rapid pace. It seemed to be a time of an intense learning curve. I went to workshops to sharpen skills, to learn and then I practised and painted with all my heart.

It seems like things were all vertical for progress from the summer of 2004 and onward. I've been blessed in so many things with art work. I wonder sometimes if it isn't that I needed to be shaped a little, deepened in my faith and have things mature in me in order to be ready. There is a line here that I want to clarify. I do not believe that God planned to have me be infertile so that I would have to go through getting children and having them taken away from me, I believe He is loving and kind and the standard Father figure. What I do think is that I needed shaping and so,

He did not stand in the way of life throwing me some hard knocks. A light was shone on some very dark and ugly things inside of me. I had not even realized they were there. They needed to be dealt with for me to grow. He has always been there. He knew how much I could handle and in the end of all that, rewarded me in some beautiful ways for keeping my faith in Him as my strength to get through it.

The bad things in life can define you in a bad way. Bitter, angry, disappointed. I have felt each and every one of those characters present themselves to me and ask to take up permanent residence. I cannot say I chased them away immediately, but they were not allowed to stay. I had to decide how I wanted to live.

My mind is a whirling mix
Of good, bad, anxious
Thankful,
Observant, oblivious
Kind and selfish
Thoughts.
I need to get settled\centered and calm.
One consistent mixture
One smooth tasteful solution
No more worry
Toss out the overwhelmed
Add extra grace
Stir in a concentrated
Cup of
Focus on God
Let sit and marinate
Sample and know
That
God is good.

15

Thankful but Expectant

I have battled in my mind over my prayers sometimes and wondered if they were indeed appropriate. Was I self-seeking and demanding? Was I just a spoiled child who didn't just say thank you for the gift, but still wanted more?

Think about this picture. A baby boy is learning to walk. The parents are kneeling on the floor with him and cheering him on as he takes his first wobbly steps. He is so pleased with himself! They are delighted and so thankful that their little child is healthy, strong and making all those first steps in life at the expected times and pace.

They also believe he will advance beyond this milestone towards another and another as he grows up. What is the difference in that and being thankful for daily provisions, but also being sure of more and better yet to come? It is the same! We can and should be most grateful for the necessities and perks we are blessed with day to day. Absolutely! We should not be content to just stay there and settle down comfortable to always and only get that far. Nope. Walk, then stride, then jog and then flat out run! That's my visual for the morning!

16

It's about Relationships

*W*hen I think about hope, and what I'd like to see sometimes, I confess I can get a little materialistic and small-minded. I want to *never* be anxious about money again. I'd like to have enough to be able to consistently give when I see a need. Make a huge difference with a contribution! I'd like to travel, to have the little luxuries in life that are just kind of sweet, like a piece of land, some horses, a log house, and a front porch...all mortgage free! I'd like to have a vehicle parked out front that is also, of course, paid for in full and is reliable and maybe even kind of cool too, like a sporty jeep! I want to send my son to the school of his choosing when he is done with high school and I do panic at how soon that will be and how I don't feel ready yet to do that for him. I don't want him to be held back by my lack of funds.

BUT Ramona, these are things and not what life is all about. They are my little wish list. When it comes to things that really truly matter though, I can see that to God, it is all about relationships.

When I write my artist newsletter that I mail out several times a year, it is like a walk down a memory lane with each person. I remember how it is I came to know them. I remember our relationship! It does good things to my heart as an artist as I recall some of them not thinking they could afford a piece of art that they'd fallen for, but how we figured something out so they could go home with it. Both their hearts and mine being full because it was so much more than a sale that day. I felt rich and blessed by seeing how they treasured something I'd painted. We became friends and stayed in touch.

My newsletters came along when I realized that my annual Christmas card list was getting ridiculous. I had this insatiable desire to write a personal letter inside each card and so the process would take weeks and my hand would have terrible writer's cramp! The newsletter allows me to keep in touch, but be a bit more practical and get to many people at a time, and then, if emails come in afterward, I can respond to those individually. It has carried on the relationships that were more than sales. I love my clients. Some of the most amazing people have entered my life since God blessed me with this business of showing and selling my art work.

It seems there is a marriage between the importance of doing something well, but then loving people and sharing your story, and hearing theirs. It makes life rich. It's a good marriage!

Friends

We need so many kinds
We need the kind who is a good listener
But when they speak, they offer wise Words
Even if few.
We need fun friends
Those who are spontaneous and free
Who make you get out of your comfort Space
And do crazy things that
You are glad you did.
We need challengers
Those who point out areas that you Have\let
become patterns in your life, in Your behavior
But shouldn't be allowed to remain that Way.
We need faithful friends
Who are always there
Even if you are far away
You know you'll never lose
Their loyalty and love.
Dependent are we
To be nurtured and grown
As independent as we think
We might be
Without love
And kindness
We are like a plant behind
Drawn curtains.
They can survive...if still
Given water and nutrients
And if maybe a crack of sunlight
Gets through. They can even live
In darkness
But they do not grow.
They never flourish into something

67

Full and beautiful.
Sprouts and offshoots can
Never be taken from them
To make others.
That's how we are as well.
Let the sunlight of friendships
Into your heart.
Open the curtains up
Move to a different window if you
Must and make the effort
Because you need
To grow and become beautiful.

17

Keep Pride in your Pocket with the Lint and other Useless things

Sometimes, I find myself wondering if I should tell clients I have in the art world, or magazine editors doing a feature on my work that I also wait tables now. Will they think that I'm not successful enough as an artist to pay attention to? I mean, the local people know of course because I'm serving them food each day. They are surrounded by the paintings and giclees on the walls that I've pretty much taken over since working there!

I wonder if they'd be more inclined to be buying the art off the walls if they were to see the pieces in a gallery or meet me at a show. These are all second guessing questions. I *have* sold pieces off the wall in the restaurant. I have gotten commissions for new pieces because of the art work on the restaurant walls and talking to the customers there for a meal. When I start letting these thoughts come at me, I give myself a little wakeup call. God is gentle, but firm with me. The wakeup call reminds me that I am there today because it is where I need to be. It is a job provided for me, to meet our needs. It has put food on our table and paid bills. Added to that, it has kept me from living a solitary existence in my studio in a new town.

Living inside my head while going through a divorce wouldn't have been good for me. Getting out, being busy, mingling with people, meeting new friends, learning a new skill, that is good for me! Pretentious pride is not good for me! So, I am saying it loud, in print for all to read! I wait tables five to six days a week. I paint whenever I'm not there. I look so forward to those studio times and cherish them more than I ever did before, but the restaurant is a good job.

I actually wish everyone could work in one for a time, if not just to appreciate the servers, cooks and dishwashers in a new way. It's hard work. It is a family restaurant owned by my brother and sister-in-law and we work together a lot of the time and enjoy that camaraderie, as well as other staff that I've come to know since moving here. People in this town have encouraged me greatly through their friendly words and generosity.

Strangers have become friends simply by my serving them their coffee and food, and taking time to talk. I go back to, "It's about relationships".

I am quite certain that I will not always live here and do what I am currently doing. It's for a season and I will do it with the best of my ability. I will also pray for more and better ability! I am learning something through this trek of life. It is how you do what you do...not simply what you do.

I hope that you have found some encouragement, some challenges and some ideas through this book. I want to fill you with hope. If you have felt like your circumstances are less than ideal, don't wait to get started on pursuing your dreams. Keep dreaming; keep working towards those desires that are planted in you. Also though, remember to fully live, today. You are being shaped and sometimes pruned. All these times in the wilderness, or moments of sadness and despair, will not last forever. I do believe in the individual plans for each of us.

We are not designed to just live and die. We are designed to crawl, walk, run... grow and fully embrace our inner gifting and have a fully alive existence.

Have you ever stood on the top of a mountain that took half the day to climb up? When you get to the top and look out over the view, that's a fully alive moment. That's when you breathe deeper, see far out beyond one foot in front of the other distance.

I encourage you to spend some time talking to God. Share with Him your thoughts, your wishes, your longings. Nothing you tell Him will surprise Him, but He desires relationship with you. That's the reason you live. I firmly believe that it is the safest place to be. Ask Him to give you direction in your life. Tell Him about your troubles and ask for wisdom and help. Remember the Proverbs... read the book! Read one chapter a day (there are thirty-one, so it's a perfect monthly project), but then repeat. Take notes of the insights that leap out at you as you do this. So many questions are answered in this book, and you'll start to see a pattern ... "If you do this, God will do this." There are principles and standards to be kept and very good things happen when you begin to apply them in your life.

Blessings and Joy on all who are holding this book in your hands right now. Thank you for taking the time, and may the coming year be one of straight up vertical growth for you! May you make your gravel pit or sandy place simply glowing and beautiful!

My precious time alone with God
In the summer, it is out on my garden Bench
In the morning sun,
Flowers and butterflies in the garden Beside me.
In the winter, it is in the fireplace room
Warmth and crackling sounds
Bringing instant comfort
And the coffee, and lately the reading Glasses, my
Bible, pen, journal
All things that are set aside as Preparations and
invitation
For God to meet with me.
I can read stories that record
Others who knew Him. Those who
Show me lessons that I hopefully can
Learn by just reading and not
By the same adversity or mistakes.
Some show me God's mercy
When they went off course, but came Back.
My course is set for the day.
In my spirit, I am settled and centered
Ready for the rest of what comes
I love to begin my day
With time alone with God.

Final Chapter
"New Beginnings"

Many months have gone by since beginning this book. As I sit in front of the computer editing it for publishing, I have bags of wedding decorations on the floor in the office. My bookshelves are bare because I am getting married in July and moving to live with the love of my life! I love the story of Ruth in the Bible because I have prayed for a "Boaz" man and that is what God has brought to me.

My little stone house on Clover Avenue has sold, and plans are taking shape.

When 2010 ended, I was standing at the beginning of a dark and uncertain future, heading down a road I had not been on before. God has been the one constant in my life. He has never left me. Family, of course, was a blanket of comfort to me and a safety net, but even there it was God who showed them how to love and help me as they did.

Life is turning a new page once again, and although this is the final chapter of this book, it is a new beginning for me. My son has plans for his final year of high school, and my fiancé's young, adult children are also at places in life where they are making big decisions for their futures. Lots of excitement and a little nervousness!

Our Father has plans for us all. Plans to prosper and not harm us. Plans for hope and a future. Jeremiah 29:11.

Let's hold fast to that promise. Believe it is true for us, because God is not a man that He would lie. I see it manifested over and over as I look back and recall all the answered prayers.

I love His plans for me. They are bigger and better than any I dared to dream on my own.

His plans for you are wonderful. If it's tough now, remember, it's the middle of your story, not the ending.

Thank you for taking the time to read this book, and if you have been encouraged in your walk, then it was a success.

"Poppies in the Sand" for me, was a tribute to God for all His many answers to prayer and provisions for me. Retelling the stories is like building little altars to always be a reminder so that in the future, I will not worry. I can know my Father is faithful and will always be my source, my strength and friend.

To see some of my paintings, please visit my website at www.swiftfox.ca. There you can find the large waterfall I wrote about called "Healing Waters". This is located through clicking on the link called "Commissions".

I love to collaborate with clients on feature pieces for their homes.

Where things go from here, I'm excited to find out. New beginnings are always a fun adventure!

Blessings and joy!
Ramona Swift-Thiessen
www.swiftfox.ca \ ramona@swiftfox.ca

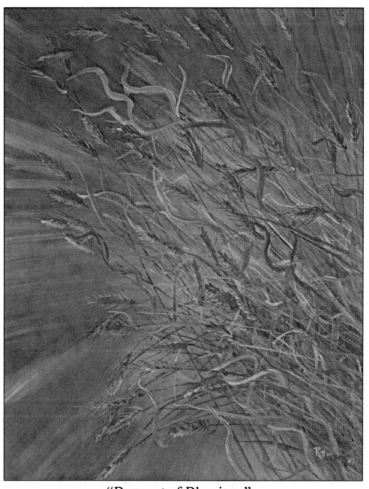

"Bouquet of Blessings"

Cary and Ramona

Cary bringing in the horses

Our wedding Day!

CPSIA information can be obtained at www.ICGtesting.com
Printed in the USA
LVOW042020250113

317306LV00001B/22/P

9 781624 190254